30-Day Journey

with Martin Luther King Jr.

30-Day Journey

with Martin Luther King Jr.

Compiled and Edited by Jonathan Chism

Fortress Press

Minneapolis

Passages

Day 1: Martin Luther King Jr., "The Power of Nonviolence," in *I Have a Dream: Writings and Speeches That Changed the World*, ed. James M. Washington (New York: HarperCollins, 1992), 31–32. © 1957 Dr. Martin Luther King Jr. © renewed 1985 Coretta Scott King.

Day 2: Martin Luther King Jr., "Antidotes for Fear," in *Strength to Love* (Philadelphia, PA: Fortress Press, 2010), 126. ©1962 Dr. Martin Luther King Jr. © renewed 1990 Coretta Scott King.

Day 3: Martin Luther King Jr., "Letter from a Birmingham Jail," in *I Have a Dream*, 94. © 1963 Dr. Martin Luther King Jr. © renewed 1991 Coretta Scott King.

Day 4: King, "Shattered Dreams," in *Strength to Love*, 94. ©1963 Dr. Martin Luther King Jr.
© renewed 1991 Coretta Scott King.

Day 5: King, "Loving Your Enemies," in *Strength to Love*, 44. © 1957 Dr. Martin Luther King Jr. ©1985 Coretta Scott King.

Day 6: Martin Luther King Jr., "Address to the First Montgomery Improvement Association (MIA) Mass Meeting," in *A Call to Conscience: The Landmark Speeches of Dr. Martin Luther King, Jr.*, ed. Clayborne Carson and Kris Shepard (New York: Warner, 2001), 11. © 1956 Dr. Martin Luther King Jr. © renewed 1984 Coretta Scott King.

Day 7: King, "Letter from a Birmingham Jail," in *I Have a Dream*, 94. © 1963 Dr. Martin Luther King Jr. © renewed 1991 Coretta Scott King.

Day 8: Martin Luther King Jr. "Where Do We Go from Here?," *Stride toward Freedom* (Boston: Beacon, 2010), 191. ©1967 Dr. Martin Luther King Jr. © renewed 1995 Coretta Scott King.

Day 9: Martin Luther King Jr., "Beyond Vietnam," April 4, 1967, Riverside Church, New York City. © 1967 Dr. Martin Luther King Jr. © 1995 Coretta Scott King.

Day 10: King, "The Birth of a New Nation," in *A Call to Conscience*, 32. © 1957 Dr. Martin Luther King Jr. © 1985 Coretta Scott King.

Day 11: Martin Luther King Jr., "The World House," in *The Radical King: Martin Luther King, Jr.*, ed. Cornel West (Boston: Beacon, 2015), 86. © 1967 Dr. Martin Luther King Jr. © 1995 Coretta Scott King.

Day 27: King, "The Power of Nonviolence" in *I Have a Dream*, 30–31. © 1957 Dr. Martin Luther King Jr. © renewed 1985 Coretta Scott King.

Day 28: King, "Paul's Letter to American Christians," in *Strength to Love*, 151. © 1956 Dr. Martin Luther King Jr. © renewed 1984 Coretta Scott King.

Day 29: King, "The Drum Major Instinct," in *I Have a Dream*, 182, 191. © 1968 Dr. Martin Luther King Jr. © renewed 1996 Coretta Scott King.

Day 30: King, "Paul's Letter to American Christians," in *Strength to Love*, 152. © 1956 Dr. Martin Luther King Jr. © renewed 1984 Coretta Scott King.

Contents

Injustice anywhere is a threat to justice everywhere. We are caught in an inescapable network of mutuality, tied in a single garment of destiny. Whatever affects one directly, affects all indirectly.

— Martin Luther King Jr.,
"Letter from a Birmingham Jail"

Introduction

Reverend Dr. Martin Luther King Jr. (1929–1968) is arguably the most renowned leader of the modern civil rights movement. His rearing in the church and extensive educational training at Morehouse College, Crozer Theological Seminary, and Boston University prepared and equipped him to become an influential ministerial activist. Overall, his deep commitment to advancing the social gospel and the kingdom of God has inspired and continues to enthuse Christians in their pursuit of justice.

King emerged as a popular civil rights leader when he accepted the invitation to lead the Montgomery Bus Boycott in December 1955. Numerous black citizens protested segregation on Montgomery buses by boycotting the buses for nearly an entire year. Black churches in Montgomery held mass meetings and lifted the spirits of blacks during the boycott as they carpooled and walked to destinations. The boycott was successful and gave momentum to the civil rights movement. Shortly after the boycott ended, King founded and was elected as the first president of the Southern Christian Leadership Conference. Drawing on Scripture and Christian principles and the teachings of Mahatma Gandhi, the organization orchestrated nonviolent protest demonstrations throughout the United States, especially the South, for more than a decade.

King received wide commendations for his "I Have A Dream" speech during the March on Washington in 1963. He won the Nobel Peace Prize and was *Time*'s person of the year in 1964. In the twenty-first century, people far and wide celebrate King as a hero. However, during his life, he received hate mail and death threats, as well as backlash from the establishment because he dared to trouble the status quo. Nevertheless, he maintained an unwavering commitment to his Christian faith, which centered on love in its various contours and expressions.

Over the next thirty days, we will engage excerpts collected from a wide range of King's sermons and writings. The bulk of the quotations include King's thoughts and reflections concerning love, including what it means to love God, oneself, and others. Throughout this journey, we will be challenged to acknowledge our human limitations and how challenging it is to reach the high standard of love that God has set for us. We have all fallen short.

Many of the selected quotes show King's conviction that receiving God's love is indispensable to overcoming fear, hopelessness, despair, bitterness, and disillusionment. No matter how long we have been on the Christian journey, we perpetually need God's love to reckon with adversity, misfortune, and challenging circumstances. Because life ebbs and flows and has its ups and downs, we cannot merely depend on the grace that we received from God yesterday. We need to receive strength from God daily (Lamentations 3:22–23). We have to recognize our daily need to receive sustenance from God's table and drink from the fountain of grace or else we risk finding ourselves spiritually famished, dehydrated, and burnt out. God's love rejuvenated King during the civil rights movement. The abiding presence of God can bring us hope, peace, joy, perspective, power, and fulfillment (Psalm 16:11). On this thirty-day journey, I anticipate that you will find a sense of renewal as you pause to embrace God's comforting presence.

It is not enough to be cognizant of our perpetual need to receive God's love; we must also share God's love with others. During this journey, King will invite us to share love through forgiving and reconciling with individuals who have injured us, through justice, through standing for righteousness, through being nonconformists, through refusing to cooperate with evil, and through sincerely and passionately devoting our lives to pursing God's will and vision for the world despite the costs. King profoundly influenced the world through demonstrating love in action. God calls us to do the same.

The quotes and reflections in this volume capture King's reflections on what it means for us to receive and extend God's love. Take note that many of the quotes come from sermons that King delivered. As a

Christian minister, King frequently quoted from the Bible, and he spent much time studying and listening for God's voice in the Scriptures. I encourage you to spend some quiet time reflecting and meditating on the Scriptures as King did. On this journey, let us open our hearts to receive God's love in various dimensions and listen to how God invites us to extend our hands of mercy and grace to others in myriad ways.

Days 1-30

Agape is understanding, creative, redemptive good will for all men . . . it is the love of God working in the minds of men. It is an overflowing love which seeks nothing in return. And when you come to love on this level you begin to love men not because they are likeable, not because they do things that attract us, but because God loves them and here we love the person who does the evil deed while hating the deed that the person does. It is the type of love that stands at the center of the movement that we are trying to carry on in the Southland—*agape*.

Reflection

Loving our friends and people that we are attracted to represents an easy, lower level of love. Loving people that we dislike is harder and reflects the highest level of love: *agape* love. This type of love denotes the selfless, abundant, abiding, and unconditional love of God. King and other Christian activists were able to "love on this level" during the civil rights era because they experienced God's love.

On this first day of our journey, I invite you to embrace, remember, and appreciate the special love God has for us. Rather than judging and condemning us, God graciously understands our flaws and human limitations. Absolutely nothing can ever separate us from God's deep love.

Consider this: to revolutionize the world through extending agape love, we must first embrace and be filled with deep gratitude for God's abundant and overflowing love. We must recognize and remember how much God loves us and desires for us to live and abide in his love.

Envy, jealousy, a lack of self-confidence, a feeling of insecurity, and a haunting sense of inferiority are all rooted in fear. We do not envy people and then fear them; first we fear them and subsequently we become jealous of them. Is there a cure for these annoying fears that pervert our personal lives? Yes, a deep and abiding commitment to the way of love. "Perfect love casteth out fear."

Reflection

Fear is a pervasive force in our lives and social world. Fear drives us to be envious, jealous, insecure, hateful, spiteful, and apathetic. It is the root cause of many human conflicts. The way of fear influences us to live beneath ourselves, stifles God's vision for our lives and our world, and causes us to become bitter. To overcome our toxic fears, we need perfect love. Perfect love does not equate to being perfect individuals. It simply means committing to a new rule in life or a radical lifestyle change: the way of love. Consider this: Perfect love means being patient with others and recognizing that we all are works in progress. It means striving to be kind and respectful to every person we encounter. It means recognizing the tremendous value of every person and seeing them as an end rather than as a means to an end.

I must admit I was initially disappointed at being so categorized. But as I continued to think about the matter I gradually gained a bit of satisfaction from being considered an extremist. Was not Jesus an extremist for love—"Love your enemies, bless them that curse you, do good to them that hate you, and pray for them which despitefully use you, and persecute you." . . . So the question is not whether we will be extremists, but what kind of extremists we will be. Will we be extremists for hate or for love?

After police arrested him for violating an injunction, King wrote his well-known "Letter from a Birmingham Jail" to influential white clergy in Alabama who publicly critiqued his demonstrations as too extreme and untimely. They argued that he was provoking social unrest and held that he should patiently work through the courts and the political system to improve race relations. In this excerpt, King clarifies the radical nature of Christian faith and witness.

Reflection

Moderation is typically promoted over extremism. Being labeled as an extremist is rarely good. Consulting a thesaurus, there are not a lot of admirable synonyms for extremism. Who wants to be painted as a fanatic, a radical, a dogmatist, or a diehard? Jesus was unapologetically fanatical, radical, dogmatic, and diehard when it came to his witness of love. His love was so radical that he loved his enemies. He fanatically loved the outcasts, the despised, and the marginalized of his society. His love was so extreme that he literally sacrificed his life for the salvation and redemption of all humanity. Consider this: for followers of Christ, loving in moderation is simply not enough; it is God's will that we strive to be and become love extremists. Like King, let us learn to rejoice and take pride in being labeled as extremists for love.

We must accept finite disappointment, but we must never lose infinite hope. Only in this way shall we live without the fatigue of bitterness and the drain of resentment.

In the introduction to this sermon titled "Shattered Dreams," King explains how Paul, the apostle to the gentiles, was enthusiastic and hopeful about carrying the gospel to Spain and fellowshipping with Roman Christians once he returned to Rome (Romans 15:24). Paul did not fulfill his desires. The Roman government arrested Paul and later executed him, yet he never lost hope or faith. In today's quote, King helps us learn to grapple with inevitable disappointment.

Reflection

King admonishes us to accept that not all of our hopes and dreams will be fulfilled in this life. There will be many times that we will not receive what we want, when we want it, and how we want it. We will have personal failures, and we may be victims of unfair social systems. While it is natural to feel frustrated with disappointment, we must not become stuck in self-pity, become resentful of others, or lose faith in God.

Being conscious that we are the beloved sons and daughters of God helps us process disappointment. We can accept finite disappointment by clinging to the infinite hope that God loves and desires what is best for us. Consider this: we must trust that the eternal God will never abandon us but will be with us always and to the end of the world.

I am certain that Jesus understood the difficulty inherent in the act of loving one's enemy. He never joined the ranks of those who talk glibly about the easiness of the moral life. He realized that *every genuine expression of love grows out of a consistent and total surrender to God.* . . . Our responsibility as Christians is to discover the meaning of this command and seek passionately to live it out in our daily lives.

Reflection

Jesus commanded that his followers not only love their friends and family members but also their enemies, haters, and backbiters. This challenging command gets at the core of the Christian faith. As King admonishes us to reflect on what this commandment means and signifies, reflect on these questions: Why does God want us to love our enemies? How does this commandment reflect God's divine nature? How do we love our enemies?

God desires for us to love our enemies because God loves all human beings unconditionally. God sends rain on both the righteous and unrighteous. God willingly forgives our sins and recognizes our worth despite our flaws. God desires to empower us to see the good and redeemable qualities within our enemies. Consider this: to love our enemies, we have to consistently and totally surrender to the source of love. God can enable us to love our enemies by helping us see them as fellow members of the human family and children of God who are worthy of our respect, compassion, and understanding.

But I want to tell you this evening that it is not enough for us to talk about love, love is one of the pivotal points of the Christian faith. There is another side called justice. And justice really is love in calculation. Justice is love correcting that which revolts against love.

King extemporaneously delivered a sermon at Holt Street Baptist Church in Montgomery, Alabama, on December 5, 1955, during the first mass meeting of the Montgomery Improvement Association. In this excerpt, he reminds his listeners how their resistance against the segregated bus system in Montgomery was upheld by Christian principles, especially love and justice.

Reflection

What does it mean to seek and obtain justice? The belief that justice centers on ensuring that criminals are locked up and punished gave birth to mass incarceration and skyrocketing rates of imprisonment for black and brown individuals. This improper conception of justice, upheld by many Christians throughout the post-civil rights era, is disconnected from agape love and leads to injustice.

King gives us a beautiful working definition of justice. He defines justice as "love in calculation" and "love correcting that which revolts against love." Justice is boldly and prophetically challenging persons, forces, and systems that are consciously or unconsciously diametrical to God's love. Rooted in love, justice is not self-serving and seeks not to crush perpetrators of injustice but to heal, mend, and restore them through love. Consider this: God calls and commands us to be calculating, intentional, focused, and strategic in our efforts to pursue justice through love. Love is always at the forefront of justice.

Will we be extremists for the preservation of injustice or for the extension of justice?

In his classic "Letter from a Birmingham Jail," King justifies his radical, nonviolent, direct-action approach to prominent white clergy by elucidating and emphasizing the extreme nature of Christian faith and witness. On day 3, we discussed how King challenges us to be extremists for love. In this quote, he invites us to commit to being extremists for justice.

Reflection

Profits, power, and the maintenance of certain privileges can tempt and influence us to be complicit with systems of injustice. To put it simply, we obtain privileges from our ties to hierarchical social arrangements and structural systems based on race, sex, class, sexual orientation, and so on.

Another way of posing King's question is to ask, Will we work to maintain privilege or become committed to extending justice? King frequently quoted the prophet Amos, who admonished the Jewish people "to let justice run down like waters and righteousness like a mighty stream." Amos castigated his fellow Jews who exploited the poor on one hand and gave sacrifices and offerings to God on the other. He told them God despised their festivals and rejected their sacrificial offerings because they upheld and condoned injustice. Consider this: to be right with God, we must reckon with our complicity in oppressive systems and choose to advance justice for all, even if it means that we lose privileges and benefits. We cannot be right with God if we participate in the preservation of injustice.

Human progress is neither automatic nor inevitable. Even a superficial look at history reveals that no social advance rolls in on the wheels of inevitability. Every step toward the goal of justice requires sacrifice, suffering, and struggle; the tireless exertions and passionate concern of dedicated individuals.

King wrote *Stride toward Freedom* following the Montgomery Bus Boycott. Today's quote resonates with the title of the book as the struggle toward freedom and justice is very much akin to a runner taking strides in a long marathon race. Despite fatigue, runners keep moving and pressing toward the finish line.

Reflection

Freedom struggles are more akin to marathon races than sprints. The histories of Native Americans, women, blacks, Latinx, disabled individuals, and the LGBTQ community signal that any meaningful expansions of freedom and justice come as a result of the efforts and sacrifices of human beings over time. If we expect social advances to happen without proactive and strategic planning, we are engaging in wishful thinking. Similarly, if we anticipate that pervasive social change will come quickly, we will become disillusioned. In this quote, King encourages us to continue to take steps toward the goal of justice.

Furthermore, we cannot pursue justice alone. Although King received much acclaim for his leadership of the movement, especially given his assassination, he did not struggle alone. Numerous individuals worked with him. Consider this: we can step closer to a more socially just world through recruiting others to stride with us. We should be mindful of our continuity with our forerunners, who participated in the long race for freedom before us. Let us celebrate the strides we have made and are making on this long journey toward freedom and justice.

When I took up the cross I recognized its meaning. It is not something that you merely put your hands on. It is not something that you wear. The cross is something that you bear and ultimately that you die on. The cross may mean the death of your popularity. It may mean the death of your bridge to the White House. It may mean the death of a foundation grant. It may cut your budget down a little, but take up your cross and bear it.

In 1967, King was criticized by the media, the white and black press, and even black civil rights organizations for condemning the Vietnam War as an unjust war. Some leaders suggested that King should stay focused on civil rights. In this excerpt from "Beyond Vietnam," an antiwar speech King delivered at Riverside Church in New York on April 4, 1967, King defends his moral stance on the Vietnam War through reflecting on what it means for Christians to carry the cross of Jesus Christ.

Reflection

As Christians, we celebrate that Jesus died to save the world and to advance the kingdom of God. Many of us demonstrate our faith through adorning the cross on necklaces and trinkets. The images of the cross remind us of Jesus's sacrificial love. In this excerpt, King reminds us that Christ calls for us to bear the cross through sacrificing ourselves for others. King believed that advancing God's justice in the world results in backlash and persecution. Echoing Thomas Shepherd's hymn, he held Jesus should not "bear the cross alone and all the world go free . . . there's a cross for ev'ry one." Consider this: neither Jesus nor King carried their crosses alone. Jesus fainted and needed help with his cross. God wills that we help each other with our burdens and uplift each other as we endure persecution when striving for righteousness and peace.

But let's be sure that our hands are clean in this struggle. Let us never fight falsehood with violence and hate and malice, but always fight with love.

Reflection

Sometimes it's tempting to fight fire with fire. It is a natural human instinct to retaliate. King reminds us that "hate and malice" can drive us to seek retribution, vengeance, and punishment rather than justice. To seek justice out of the purity of love and to take the higher road, we need God to cleanse our hearts. We must be careful not to lose sight of love as we seek justice. We cannot advance the struggle for justice and overcome evil without creatively using the weapon of love. Consider this: civil rights activists creatively fought injustice by using nonviolent tactics and demonstrations as weapons of love. I challenge you to consider other creative ways we might fight social evil through employing the powerful weapon of love.

The universe is so structured that things go awry if men are not diligent in their cultivation of the other-regarding dimension. "I" cannot reach fulfillment without "thou." The self cannot be self without other selves. Self-concern without other-concern is like a tributary that has no outward flow to the ocean. Stagnant, still and stale, its lacks both life and freshness.

King wrote his last book, *Where Do We Go from Here? Chaos or Community*, while in Jamaica. He disconnected himself from movement concerns and took time to write and reflect. In this quote, King shares a global vision for social justice. He held that nonviolent direct action could be employed to combat racism, poverty, and militarism throughout the world.

Reflection

Preoccupation with agendas, calendars, and goals is often encouraged and viewed as a good thing. Common advice encourages you to think about yourself first. The expectation in this competitive world is that others are thinking about themselves. Selfishness is dangerous when it influences us to disregard and isolate ourselves from others.

King reminds us that it is imperative to respect and cooperate with others throughout the universe. Consider this: From the moment that we come into this world to the day we die, we need others in order to experience fulfillment, completeness, and the beauty of life. Not only do we need other human beings, we also need healthy ecosystems to survive and thrive on this planet. We can live the best life by regarding the needs of others in all their variety and by recognizing our need to collaborate with diverse groups and people.

The rich man was a fool because he failed to realize his dependence on others.... A victim of the cancerous disease of egotism, he failed to realize that wealth always comes as a result of the commonwealth.... He failed to realize that he was an heir of a vast treasury of ideas and labor to which both the living and the dead contributed.

Reflection

In this excerpt from a sermon, King unpacks a parable about a certain rich man deemed by Christ to be a fool. On the surface, the average person might judge the rich man to be a wise man. He had an excellent financial plan. The rich man was preparing to retire, enjoy a comfortable lifestyle, and reap the benefits of his hard labor. How was this seemingly wise man a fool?

King helps us see that the rich man was a fool because he did not possess gratitude for the countless persons who invested in him over the years. He arrogantly perceived that he had pulled himself up by his own bootstraps, and he embraced the popular myth of being a self-made man. Consider this: the rich man's foolishness ultimately comes from his failure to recognize the meaning and measure of true wealth: being invested in the commonwealth, serving God through serving others with a humble and grateful heart.

The call for a world-wide fellowship that lifts neighborly concern beyond one's tribe, race, class and nation is in reality a call for an all-embracing and unconditional love for all men.

On April 4, 1967, King addressed an organization called Clergy and Laity Concerned about Vietnam at Riverside Church in New York. In this brief excerpt from his speech, King responds to critics who insisted that he should remain focused on fighting for civil rights in the United States instead of being concerned about injustice in Vietnam.

Reflection

The prosperity of our families, communities, and nations depends on the unselfish contributions of their various members. Similarly, the world cannot flourish unless the various societies and nations work together in peace and love. King challenges us to have a global vision and to recognize that we are world citizens and members of a "world-wide fellowship." Despite our different religions, economic systems, and worldviews, King believed that citizens throughout the world could love one another and work together. Consider this: King did not restrict the love of God to any particular religion or nation. The love of God is pervasive and "all-encompassing." God wills that people of all faiths, views, and cultures love each other.

Injustice anywhere is a threat to justice everywhere. We are caught in an inescapable network of mutuality, tied in a single garment of destiny. Whatever affects one directly, affects all indirectly.

This is a popular quotation from King's "Letter from a Birmingham Jail." As King and Southern Christian Leadership Conference (SCLC) activists protested injustices in various states, Southern whites frequently accused them of being "outside" agitators. Since King lived in Atlanta, Georgia, white clergy in Alabama accused King of coming to Birmingham, Alabama, to stir up dissension. In this quote, King explains and justifies his rationale and first-amendment right to protest segregation in Birmingham.

Reflection

We should not become comfortable with passively accepting injustice outside of our spheres. Throughout the civil rights movement, King and members of SCLC showed up at various locations throughout the South to protest injustice because King recognized that what happened in Birmingham affected him in Atlanta as well as blacks throughout the South. Even more, King knew the segregation laws and customs in Birmingham negatively impacted the health of the United States. By using the words *everywhere* and *all*, King refers to people beyond the borders of the United States and throughout the world. He believed that all human life is connected and intertwined and that we should be ready to challenge injustice anywhere in the world.

Consider this: injustice that happens beyond our immediate circles is our business because our lives and futures are intertwined. If we turn a blind eye to injustice and are insensitive to the plight of marginalized and oppressed people locally and globally, we ultimately endanger our own well-being and future generations.

We must rapidly begin the shift from a "thing"-oriented society to a "person"-oriented society. When machines and computers, profit motives and property rights are considered more important than people, the giant triplets of racism, materialism and militarism are incapable of being conquered.

Today's quote comes from the concluding chapter of King's last book, *Where Do We Go from Here: Chaos of Community.* Toward the end of his life, King began to broaden his focus beyond civil rights for blacks in the United States. He reflected deeply on injustices that were taking place around the globe and held there was an urgent need to change course.

Reflection

Who doesn't like or want nice and beautiful things—the latest smartphone, a new car, designer clothes? Certainly, there is no problem with enjoying nice things, but King emphasizes that we should prioritize human beings. King envisaged that if people continued to be overly preoccupied with material possessions and the preservation of power and privilege, then the future of human society and civilization was in jeopardy. Given the advancements in technology and military weaponry that occurred in the twentieth century and the threat of nuclear warfare that existed during the Cold War era, King stressed that we must have a sense of urgency and "rapidly" change course to overcome forces that threaten the future well-being of all humans and our planet. Consider this: the stakes are still high in our contemporary period. We must not be passive and apathetic and allow bigotry, greed, and militarism to prevail. Our collective future still hinges on shifting our values and priorities. We must deeply value people over profits.

Many people have been plunged into the abyss of emotional fatalism because they did not love themselves properly. So every individual has a responsibility to be concerned about himself enough to discover what he is made for. After he discovers his calling he should set out to do it with all of the strength and power in his being. He should do it as if God Almighty called him at this particular moment in history to do it. He should seek to do his job so well that the living, the dead, or the unborn could not do it better.

In this excerpt from *The Measure of a Man*, King describes John's vision of the new city of God in Revelation and insists that this city of God signifies the completeness of human life. He holds that central to living a balanced life is learning to love God, others, and ourselves. In this quote, King specifically discusses the importance and significance of self-love.

Reflection

It is easy to become so preoccupied with making ends meet and surviving that we fail to take the time to ask ourselves serious questions. This type of living is akin to floating in the vast ocean of life without a sense of direction and purpose. King challenges us to discover our purpose in life through consulting the Creator.

Discovering our purpose is only a first step. It helps us to develop confidence that we are heading in the right direction. The next step is for us to press the imaginary gas pedal of life and go full throttle toward the destination that God is leading us. Consider this: God Almighty did indeed create us to do what God has called us to do. We don't have an infinite amount of time to complete our mission in life. Let us maximize and make the most of our finite opportunities to accomplish the assignment God has given us with excellence and distinction.

Few words in the New Testament more clearly and solemnly express the magnanimity of Jesus' spirit than that sublime utterance from the cross, "Father, forgive them; for they know not what they do." This is love at its best.

Reflection

Throughout his ministry and life, Jesus not only admonished his disciples and followers to love their enemies, but he died practicing the very message he preached. Hanging from the cross, Jesus did not seek retributive justice from God. He prayed that God would forgive those who crucified him. Perhaps he was able to forgive at this excruciating moment because he understood that the people who crucified him "knew not what they do." According to King, when making this assertion, Jesus was referring to their "intellectual and spiritual blindness." He understood that they lived in darkness. He had empathy for those influenced and affected by the power of darkness. Hanging on the cross, he knew that the only way persons in darkness could see the light is through love. Consider this: when we forgive others, God is using us to help people who are spiritually blind see and experience God's love. Forgiveness is one of the key ways that we express and extend God's love and grace to others.

Non-cooperation with evil is as much a moral obligation as is cooperation with good.

In his autobiography, compiled by Clayborne Carson, King discusses how he came to embrace civil disobedience, or "the theory of nonviolent resistance," after reading Henry David Thoreau's essay "On Civil Disobedience" while attending Morehouse College in 1944. Today's quote from a sermon reflects King's understanding and moral convictions regarding civil disobedience.

Reflection

Giving to charities is a safe and noble way that we can cooperate with the greater good. As much as God desires for us to share meals with those who are poor, God also wills that we work to challenge systems that perpetuate poverty. For example, we should not be complacent with merely ministering to persons confined in jails and prisons but should challenge the unjust criminal-justice system.

King's admonition to challenge oppressive powers reminds us of our dual obligation to resist injustice and to do good. Consider this: surrendering to God's rule for love and justice includes courageously resisting and protesting evil embedded in various institutional powers and centers. This is our moral obligation.

We need to recapture the gospel glow of the early Christians, who were nonconformists in the truest sense of the word and refused to shape their witness according to the mundane patterns of the world. Willingly they sacrificed fame, fortune, and life itself in behalf of a cause they knew to be right. Quantitatively small, they were qualitatively giants.

Reflection

Nonconformity is challenging for many because of the fear of being rejected, excluded, and treated as an outcast by others. We lose our glow and radiance as the people of God when we aspire to please people rather than God. Throughout American history, we must acknowledge that many institutional churches have conformed to the desires and expectations of the populace rather than God. A cornucopia of churches have historically condoned the conquest of indigenous Americans, slavery, Jim Crow, the prison industrial complex, and the marginalization of gays and lesbians. People affiliated with a number of Christian churches held that AIDS was God's punishment for homosexuality.

Consider this: The "gospel glow" of early Christians was tied to their refusal to conform to the status quo and prevailing customs and their embrace of Christ's calling to be "the salt of the earth" and "the light of the world." They imitated Christ's example of humility and devoted themselves to God's rule of love and service to others. Though many people may have seen them as small, God saw them as great.

On some positions, Cowardice asks the question, "Is it safe?" Expediency asks the question, "Is it politic?" And Vanity comes along and asks the question, "Is it popular?" But Conscience asks the question, "Is it right?" And there comes a time when one must take a position that is neither safe, nor politic, nor popular, but he must do it because Conscience tells him it is right.

This is another quote from King's antiwar speech, "Beyond Vietnam," delivered at New York's Riverside Church on April 4, 1967. Rather than being swayed by the advice and warning of his critics to avoid protesting the Vietnam War, King stressed the importance of being guided by conscience.

Reflection

Have there been times when you failed to follow the dictates of your conscience—your inner sense of right and wrong? We may rationalize not following our conscience because doing the right thing means risking our safety, career advancement, or reputation. Cowardice, expediency, and vanity are only a few of the voices that can lead us down deleterious paths. The voices of anger, lust, greed, and pride pose questions of their own that we must be careful to guard against. God endowed us with a conscience via the gift of the Holy Spirit, which leads and direct us. Despite risks or dangers, we must follow our conscience. Consider this: if you want to ensure that God is directing your decision-making, make sure that your action is rooted in love. God will not lead us to do something that is unloving and harmful to others.

I was ready to give up. With my cup of coffee sitting untouched before me, I tried to think of a way to move out of the picture without appearing a coward. In this state of exhaustion, when my courage had all but gone, I decided to take my problem to God. With my head in my hands, I bowed over the kitchen table and prayed aloud.... The words I spoke to God that midnight are still vivid in my memory. "I am here taking a stand for what I believe is right. But now I am afraid. The people are looking to me for leadership, and if I stand before them without strength and courage, they too will falter. I am at the end of my powers. I have nothing left. I've come to the point where I can't face it alone."... It seemed as though I could hear the quiet assurance of an inner voice saying: "Martin Luther, stand up for righteousness. Stand up for justice. Stand up for truth. And lo, I will be with you. Even until the end of the world." ... He promised never to leave me alone. At that moment, I experienced the presence of the Divine as I had never experienced God before. It seemed as though I could hear the quiet assurance of an inner voice saying: "Stand up for justice, stand up for truth; and God will be at your side forever." Almost at once my fears began to go. My uncertainty disappeared. I was ready to face anything.

Reflection

We will all have moments in our lives where we feel like giving up. These are "midnight moments," times when darkness creeps in and it is difficult to trace the light of God's presence. In the midnight hour of despair and fear, like King, we must recognize our need to converse with God. During his prayer time, King became naked before God, disclosing his fears, faltering courage, fatigue, and need for help. We, too, can talk to God honestly about our fears. When we pray, God can give us the reassurance and hope we need. Most of all, being in the presence of God reminds us that we are not struggling alone. Consider this: stop pretending that things are fine and that you can handle it on your own. It is alright to cry out to God for help and strength on this journey.

During the Montgomery Bus Boycott, numerous racist individuals endeavored to intimidate and discourage King by sending him hostile letters and making menacing telephone calls, up to forty a day. In today's passage, King describes how one disturbing phone call caused him to become fearful, restless, and doubtful as to whether he should continue to lead the movement. Here, he gives details about how God renewed his courage.

This inner stability of the man of faith is Christ's chief legacy to his disciples. He offers neither material resources nor a magical formula that exempts us from suffering and persecution, but he brings an imperishable gift: "Peace I leave with you." This is that peace which passeth all understanding.

Reflection

As human beings, we often want to avoid suffering and pain. If God loves and cares for us and is all-powerful, then why would God allow us to suffer? King explains that being Christian does not equate to freedom from pain and suffering. Contrary to the prosperity gospel, God's inheritance to people of faith is not rooted in financial blessings or promises of wealth and material prosperity. Peace is a remarkable spiritual gift that comes through spending time in God's presence. King's experience with God while praying at his kitchen table enabled him to have peace even after his home was bombed during the Montgomery Bus Boycott. Consider this: we receive the peace of God through being reassured that God's love is present with us. This gift of peace can help us not fall apart amid the challenges of life.

Yes, I am personally the victim of deferred dreams, of blasted hopes, but in spite of that I close today by saying I still have a dream, because, you know, you can't give up in life. If you lose hope, somehow you lose that vitality that keeps life moving, you lose that courage to be, that quality that helps you to go on in spite of all.

In December 1967, King delivered "A Christmas Sermon on Peace" at Ebenezer Baptist Church in Atlanta, Georgia. His sermon was aired by the Canadian Broadcasting Corporation and reached an international audience. It was the conclusion to a series of five lectures King delivered in Canada as part of Massey Lectures. In the sermon, King stresses the importance of persistently pursuing freedom, justice, and world peace through nonviolent means. He encourages his congregation and the world at large to never give up.

Reflection

Unfulfilled or delayed dreams can easily lead us to feel like giving up. King could have abandoned the dream he articulated in his "I Have a Dream" speech in 1963. After his speech, white supremacist groups perpetuated hate crimes, and numerous riots occurred that reflected people's discontentment with persisting racial and economic injustice. Yet, in this sermon delivered in 1967, King was adamant, "I still have a dream." He courageously kept pushing and striving, although he never really obtained what he envisioned during his lifetime. Consider this: hope undergirded and defined who King was as a person of faith. As people of faith, hope is embedded in our DNA. Hope enables us to keep striving for things we don't see. Quoting civil rights activist Reverend Jesse Jackson, we are people who *keep hope alive.* In line with President Barack Obama, we take pride in possessing the sheer *audacity to hope.* We are people who refuse to give up on our dreams because we have hope in an unseen power greater than ourselves.

When our days become dreary with low-hovering clouds of despair, and when our nights become darker than a thousand midnights, let us remember that there is a creative force in this universe working to pull down the gigantic mountains of evil, a power that is able to make a way out of no way and transform dark yesterdays into bright tomorrows.

This excerpt is from a speech King delivered during an annual convention of the Southern Christian Leadership Conference in Atlanta, Georgia, on August 16, 1967. As SCLC president, King proudly acknowledged how the organization stood at the forefront of the struggle against segregation and for voting and economic rights during the 1950s and 1960s. Yet, he insisted that the struggle was far from complete and that SCLC members should be prepared to encounter future setbacks and bumps in the road.

Reflection

If you are like me and don't always pay attention to the weather report, you might keep an umbrella in your car or in your office to be prepared just in case it rains. In this quote, King reminds us that our days will not always be replete with victories and sunshine; the rain and thunderstorms of life are inevitable. Doubtful and gloomy days are to be expected as we strive for freedom and justice.

King reminds us that during these times we must remember and have faith that our God, the Creator, is working to combat the forces of evil in myriad ways. Consider this: we are in solidarity with the King of kings and Lord of lords, who will ultimately be victorious over all forms of evil. Our faith in divine power and victory can lift us and give us a renewed sense of hope that a brighter day is indeed coming. *Trouble will not last always.* The sun will shine again. Our God will win.

I have been tortured without and tormented within by the raging fires of tribulation. I have been forced to muster what strength and courage I have to withstand howling winds of pain and jostling storms of adversity. But as the years have unfolded the eloquently simple words of Mother Pollard have come back again and again to give light and peace and guidance to my troubled soul. "God's gonna take care of you." . . . This faith transforms the whirlwind of despair into a warm and reviving breeze of hope.

In this sermon, King describes encouragement he received from Mother Pollard, an elderly member of his congregation, after he spoke at a large meeting. Though King endeavored to preach with conviction and exude confidence before his congregation, he felt dejected and fearful after receiving death threats. Sensing that something was disturbing him, Mother Pollard talked to King and reassured him that God was with him.

Reflection

On a Monday night in 1956, Mother Pollard spoke powerful words to King that energized him at his core. Her words stuck with him throughout his life. Mother Pollard transferred her faith to King when he was feeling downhearted. Consider this: God can give us the encouragement we need through other people. It is vitally important to edify and uplift each other. God wills for us to be connected with people who can hold us accountable and encourage us in love. If we are disconnected from community, we miss the opportunity to hear God speaking through others as well as the chance for God to use us to give others the encouragement they need.

So I say to you, seek God and discover him and make him a power in your life. Without him all of our efforts turn to ashes and our sunrises into darkest nights. Without him, life is a meaningless drama with the decisive scenes missing. But with him we are able to rise from the fatigue of despair to the buoyance of hope. With him we are able to rise from the midnight of desperation to the daybreak of joy. Saint Augustine was right—we were made for God and we will be restless until we find rest in him.

Reflection

In our fast-paced, competitive, and globally connected twenty-first-century society, there are many things to distract us from focusing on our relationship with God. The hustle and bustle of pursuing our goals and agendas can make it difficult to spend time with God. Our phones, tablets, televisions, and computers give us constant access to what's happening around the world, from the national news to our friends' latest updates, as well as make us constantly available to everyone else, posing further challenges to concentrating on cultivating our relationship with God.

Failing "to seek God and discover him" will ultimately lead to feeling overwhelmed, tired, stressed, and unfulfilled. Consider this: seeking and discovering God can bring meaning, hope, and peace to our lives. As we grow in our relationship with God, our stress level will decrease, and we will learn to rest in God.

The end of violence or the aftermath of violence is bitterness. The aftermath of non-violence is reconciliation and the creation of a beloved community.

This is a quote from a sermon entitled "Birth of a New Nation," which King delivered at Dexter Avenue Baptist in Montgomery, Alabama, on April 7, 1957. In this sermon, King discussed at length Prime Minister Kwame Nkrumah's leadership of a nonviolent revolt against colonial oppression in Ghana. The struggle for independence in Ghana inspired King to have hope and optimism that the nonviolent civil rights movement could lead to reconciliation between blacks and whites in the United States.

Reflection

During the civil rights era, several black revolutionaries perceived King's nonviolent program and vision of beloved community as unrealistic. Given persisting social inequality, some may question if the United States will ever be able to fully include all of its citizens regardless of their race, sex, gender, sexual orientation, creed, and so on.

King's faith in beloved community stemmed not only from Scripture but also from history. The colonial resistance struggles in India and Africa gave King hope that beloved community was possible in the United States and throughout the world. Consider this: to maintain hope in the creation of a beloved community, let us draw inspiration from stories of reconciliation. For example, in 1972, George Wallace, the former governor of Alabama known for his staunch support for segregation, asked black congregants at Dexter Avenue Baptist Church, formerly pastored by King, to forgive him. Many persons in the congregation forgave and reconciled with Wallace. Such glimpses of beloved community can encourage us on our journey for social justice.

The end of life is not to be happy, nor to achieve pleasure and avoid pain, but to do the will of God, come what may.

This short quote comes from a sermon King delivered titled "Paul's Letter to American Christians." King imagined how the apostle Paul might encourage contemporary American Christians who were experiencing persecution for standing up for civil rights.

Reflection

Billion-dollar industries, including sports, fitness, medicine, and insurance, have developed to serve our desires for happiness, pleasure, and health. We can easily invest a tremendous amount of time and money pursuing these things throughout the course of our lives and neglecting to focus on our highest priority—pursuing God's will. Paul endured adversity because he was able to remain focused on completing God's assignment rather than his own agenda. Despite being subjected to persecution and pain, Paul testified on multiple occasions how he experienced God's grace and love. Consider this: when it is all said and done, those who serve and work for God live a life full of meaning and purpose that glorifies God. Completing God's will provides us true fulfillment.

We all want to be important, to surpass others, to achieve distinction, to lead the parade . . . this desire for distinction is the basic impulse, the basic drive of human life—this drum major instinct . . . if you want to say that I was a drum major, say that I was a drum major for justice; say that I was a drum major for peace; I was a drum major for righteousness. And all of the other shallow things will not matter. I won't have any money to leave behind. I won't have the fine and luxurious things of life to leave behind. But I just want to leave a committed life behind.

This is an excerpt from one of King's last sermons, "The Drum Major Instinct." He preached this sermon on February 4, 1968, at Ebenezer Baptist Church, roughly two months before his assassination in Memphis, Tennessee, during the Sanitation Workers Strike.

Reflection

It is natural to strive to be first, to seek to rise to the top, and to aim to win. In this sermon, King acknowledges our basic human desire for recognition and our quest for significance. It feels good to receive a distinguished award in your area of expertise.

However, King admonishes us not to become preoccupied with being perceived as successful in the eyes of other people. True greatness is rooted in living a life committed to justice, peace, and righteousness. Consider this: our ultimate aim as believers is to be distinguished in God's eyes and according to his righteous standards. We please God when we pursue justice, peace, and righteousness and push to extend his love. Through dedicating our lives to serving God and others, like King, we can lead the type of life that inspires others around us for generations.

I have discovered that the highest good is love. This principle is at the center of the cosmos. It is the great unifying force of life. God is love. He who loves has discovered the clue to the meaning of ultimate reality.

Reflection

Over the past thirty days, we have been honest about how challenging it is to love unconditionally and universally. King insists that "love is the great unifying force of life." Yet, division and conflict are rampant. Racism, sexism, classism, and homophobia persist. King deeply believed that love was the force that could unite us and save us from destroying ourselves.

As Christians, we are called to be exemplars and conduits of love. Consider this: The world desperately needs the people of God to step up and allow God's love to flow through them and to others. God can use us to be agents of healing, restoration, reconciliation, and peace in this world replete with division. May God's love infect us and spread throughout our relationships, homes, and neighborhoods, and keep spreading throughout the world.

Further Reading

Baldwin, Lewis. *Never to Leave Us Alone: The Prayer Life of Martin Luther King Jr.,* Minneapolis: Fortress Press, 2010.

———. *The Voice of Conscience: The Church in the Mind of Martin Luther King, Jr.* New York: Oxford University Press, 2010.

King, Martin Luther, Jr. *The Autobiography of Martin Luther King, Jr.* Edited by Clayborne Carson. New York: Warner, 1998.

———. *A Call to Conscience: The Landmark Speeches of Dr. Martin Luther King, Jr.* Edited by Clayborne Carson and Kris Shepard. New York: Warner, 2001.

———. *I Have a Dream: Writings and Speeches That Changed the World.* Edited by James M. Washington. New York: HarperCollins, 1992.

———. *The Measure of a Man.* Philadelphia, PA: Fortress Press, 1988.

———. *The Radical King: Martin Luther King, Jr.* Edited by Cornel West. Boston: Beacon, 2015.

———. *Strength to Love.* Philadelphia, PA: Fortress Press, 1981.

———. *Stride toward Freedom.* Boston: Beacon, 2010.

———. *Trumpet of Conscience.* San Francisco: Harper & Row, 1987.

———. *Where Do We Go from Here: Chaos or Community?* Boston: Beacon, 1968.

———. *Why We Can't Wait.* New York: Signet Classic, 2000.